MASTERPIECE

MASTERPIECE

DEANNA DELOATCH

CITI OF
BOOKS

CITIOFBOOKS, INC.
3736 Eubank NE Suite A1
Albuquerque, NM 87111-3579
www.citiofbooks.com
Hotline: 1 (877) 389-2759
Fax: 1 (505) 930-7244

Ordering Information:

Quantity sales. Special discounts are available on quantity purchases by corporations, associations, and others. For details, contact the publisher at the address above.

Printed in the United States of America.

ISBN-13:   Softcover   979-8-89391-961-5
             eBook   979-8-89391-962-2

Library of Congress Control Number: 2025920962

TABLE OF CONTENTS

Chapter 1: You are a Masterpiece 1

Chapter 2: I Don't Feel Like a Masterpiece 4

Chapter 3: Rising Above Living in your Emotions 8

Chapter 4: Masterpieces at Work and in the Community 11

Chapter 5: You are a Winner 15

Chapter 6: Understand your Anointing and Calling 20

Chapter 7: Enhance your imagination 24

Chapter 8: Conclusion 28

Acknowledgements 39

Chapter 1

You are a Masterpiece

You are a masterpiece. You are valuable. You were created in the image and likeness of God. The problem is the devil wants to tell you otherwise. The Bible says in I Peter 5:8 (NKJV), "to be sober, be vigilant, because your adversary the devil walks about like a roaring lion, seeking whom he may devour." The devil is out to get you. He is out to steal your joy, your peace, your mind. He knows if he can enter your thought life and tell you that you are a nobody and that you don't amount to anything, then you will ultimately self-destruct.

Our thoughts are the seats to our destiny. Truly they are. When I was growing up, I had teachers and guidance counselors purposely try to tell me that I was low academically and would only be a truck driver and I was not "college material." They planted these seeds in my thoughts, but instead of deterring me from achieving my goals, they only made me work harder and push further ahead. Now, four college degrees later, I look back and laugh. Yes, they meant harm, they were assigned by the enemy to frustrate me, but deep inside, I knew God had called me for greatness and that I was going to be more than a truck driver.

And so it is with you. Perhaps you are a truck driver. There is nothing wrong with the occupation. Lord, knows we need our supplies delivered on time. But perhaps you want more out of life. Perhaps you want to own the trucking company and go into business for yourself. I am here to tell you that you can do just that because you are a masterpiece. God created you in His image and likeness and breathed his breath of life into you. Isn't that neat? We have the almighty power of God's breath in us. The same breath of life that caused Moses to part the Red Sea. The same breath that raised Jesus from the dead is alive in us!

The Bible says in **Genesis 1: 26-28, "Then God said, 'Let us make man in our image, according to our likeness; let them have dominion over the fish of the sea, over the birds of the air, and over the cattle, over all the earth and over every creeping thing that creeps on the earth.' So God created man in His own image in the image of God. He created him; male and female, He created them. Then God blessed them." (Where it says "God created man in our image, " it is talking about the trinity. Jesus and the Holy Spirit were present when God created man. As Christians, we believe that God is Triune).**

So, we are made in the image of Christ and therefore, have all of the rights that He has. As Phillipians 4:13 tells us, we can do all things as He strengthens us.

For this reason, we have the spiritual DNA to open that trucking business or whatever other business we want to open. Or perhaps it is to be the best stay at home mom there has ever been. God has graced us with that ability as well. As stated before, we are His masterpiece, and as soon as we start to speak it, we will believe it. God spoke, "Let us create man," and man appeared. It began with a thought, followed by the words. Once we think it, we own it and then it comes to pass. So, I encourage you today to see yourself as a masterpiece, speak that you are a masterpiece and start living as if you are a masterpiece... because you are.

Chapter 2

I Don't Feel Like a Masterpiece

In chapter 1, I said that you are a masterpiece, and that you are created in God's image. Begin to see yourself as a masterpiece, speak that you are a masterpiece, and start living as a masterpiece. But what if you do not feel like a masterpiece?

Feelings are just that- feelings. They are emotions. They come and go. I know that I am pretty. My husband tells me that I am pretty. My mother tells me that I am pretty. I can look in the mirror and see that I am pretty (not trying to be vain), but sometimes I don't feel pretty. There are days when I will tell my sister, "Oh, sorry Diana, I don't feel like going to the movies and getting dressed up. I'm not having one of my pretty days." Or I will go to McDonalds and order large fries and medium diet Dr. Pepper, and eat and drink to my heart's content (I can be an emotional eater) because I "feel" sad.

Joyce Meyer is a great woman of God who has a lot to say about feelings and how we should master them. But before we go get one of her books to get her advice, first let's see what God has to say. Let's explore the word of God.

Getting into the Word of God to master our emotions and feelings may sound theological, but I bet it will work for you. It worked for me. The more I am into the Word, the more stable my emotions are (even with my bipolar disorder- especially with my bipolar disorder).

The word of God says in **I Samuel 28: 20, "Saul fell full-length on the ground, paralyzed with fright because of Samuel's words. He was also faint with hunger, for he had eaten nothing all day and all night. When the woman saw how distraught he was, she said, "Sir, I obeyed your command at the risk of my life. Now do what I say, and let me give you a little something to eat so you can regain your strength for the trip back."**

In this passage of scripture, Saul was so distraught because Samuel had advised him that because of his actions, David was going to take over his kingdom; that his feelings had even affected his eating habits (talk about emotional eater!). Sometimes, we can be so distressed over a situation, that it affects our eating habits. We either eat too much (as in my case) or eat too little, like Saul, and lose our strength. God doesn't want us to be emotional eaters. He wants us to have healthy appetites and take good care of our temples. He even says in **Romans 12: 1, "And so, dear brothers and sisters, I plead with you to give your bodies to God because of all he has done for you. Let them be a living and holy sacrifice- the kind he will find acceptable. This is truly the way to worship him."**

Our bodies are God's temple and rightly so, He wants us to take good care of them.

Let's see what our good friend, Joyce Meyer has to say about living beyond your feelings in her book entitled just that, "Living Beyond Your Feelings" (2011).

"Emotions are powerful, and sometimes we feel overpowered by them. According to Webster's, the root source of the word emotion is the Latin *ex-movere*, meaning "to move away." And that is exactly what emotions do. They move up from somewhere deep within us and then they move out and pressure us to follow them. An emotional person is one who tends to follow her feelings most of the time. Emotional people think, speak, and act according to feelings. God has a good plan for our lives, but we do have an enemy named Satan, and his desire is that we follow all our feelings and end up in ruin." (page 47).

Think about a situation that makes you impatient. For me, it is when I go to my mother's house to pick her up to take her to an appointment and she is not ready. My mother doesn't drive anymore, and as her primary caregiver, I do most of the driving for her to various appointments. Often, she is running behind schedule, and it takes her longer to get ready in the mornings because she uses a walker, and she is 82 years old. A lot of times, I feel very impatient and feel like yelling at her, but I know I will later regret my words and only hurt her feelings. Sometimes, I do let my feelings and emotions get the best of me and lash out. When I do, I feel so bad because I don't know how much longer I will have my mother on this earth to take her to these appointments, and she was so patient with me when I didn't drive when I was younger.

We must be ever so careful when we let our emotions and feelings get the best of us because we can say things we did not mean to say.

James 3:2-6 says, "Indeed, we all make many mistakes. For if we could control our tongues, we would be perfect and could also control ourselves in every other way. We can make a large horse go wherever we want by means of a small bit in its mouth. And a small rudder makes a huge ship turn wherever the pilot chooses to go, even though the winds are strong. In the same way, the tongue is a small thing that makes grand speeches. But a tiny spark can set a great forest on fire. And among all the parts of the body, the tongue is a flame of fire."

We can see from the above passage, that just like a forest fire, the tongue can set off flames of sayings that we didn't mean and can hurt individuals and families. That is why it is so important not to be led by our emotions and feelings so much that we say things that we later regret; instead, we must be led by the Spirit.

Yet, despite all this, God says we are still a masterpiece, and we can rise above living in our emotions.

Chapter 3

Rising Above Living in your Emotions

One way we can rise above living in our emotions is to be Spirit-led. To be Spirit-led doesn't have to be spooky spiritual, it just means we are led by the Spirit and not led by our sinful, carnal natures. What does it look like to live by our carnal nature? Well, I am glad you asked. The Bible tells us in Romans 8: 5-8:

"Those who are dominated by the sinful nature think about sinful things, but those who are controlled by the Holy Spirit think about things that please the Spirit. So, letting your sinful nature control your mind leads to death. But letting the Spirit control your mind leads to life and peace. For the sinful nature is always hostile to God. It never did obey God's laws, and it never will. That's why those who are still under the control of their sinful nature can never please God" (NLT).

Do you want to please God? If you are a Christian, your answer should be an emphatic "yes." We can see from the above passage that one way we please God is by yielding to the Holy Spirit. The process of becoming more Christ-like is known as sanctification. As we grow in our Christian Walk, it is important that we become more

Christ-like. We are not to get saved and just die and go to heaven, but we are to make disciples of others and grow up in our salvation.

For example, when you are at the grocery store, and you find yourself in the longest line, and the cashier at the checkout is in training, and you know you only have twenty minutes to get back to work, you may have a desire to get impatient and scream at the cashier and tell her how she is ruining your already short lunch break, but you must remember not to "react in the flesh," but rather, be led by the Spirit. Take a breath, smile and be courteous.

Believe me, this is not easy at first. But as you grow in being Spirit-led and walking as Christ would have you, it becomes easier. One way to do this is to stay in the Word and pray. The Word of God has a cleansing effect on us. It washes us and cleanses our mind, body, and spirit. That is why it is important to make time to pray and read your Bible daily.

Being Spirit-led in your marriage

If you are married, the person who helps you become most like Christ and aids you in the sanctification process and being Spirit-led is your spouse. The Bible says in **I Corinthians 6: 16, "The two are united into one." (NLT)**

Our spouses should point us to Christ in a Christian marriage. When I first got married, I used to be so mean to my husband. My husband has an intellectual disability and I used to get so mad at him for not handling our bills properly. I wanted him to be the head of our household and handle the finances, but he was incapable of doing this because of his disability. This used to make me argue with him a lot and I would belittle him and call him "dumb." I would do this primarily because he had told me that when he was in high school, the kids used to call him dumb, and it really hurt his feelings. I wanted him to hurt, and I took pleasure in his hurting. He, on the other hand, loved me so much unconditionally, he would just try to serve me and call me "beautiful" and pray for me. We eventually divorced and remarried a couple of years later. But I still had not learned my lesson. He started letting me handle the finances, but after about 9 months into our new marriage, I began to argue and threaten divorce again.

My husband just began to pray more intensely for me and serve me as Christ served the church. He would write in his journal every night (unbeknownst it to me until I found it years later), recording his prayers for me. I was praying for him to change and one day, the Holy Spirit spoke to my heart and said, "you need to change. You need to be more selfless." My husband's prayers were working on me.

I began to see Christ in him, and through much counseling and prayer, I began to change. Now I no longer call him dumb or speak anything negative over him. We rarely argue and we have a beautiful marriage. Our marriage is a testimony of how God can heal a relationship. I was the one who led my husband to the Lord in the beginning of our relationship, but later, he was the one who "grew me up" even more in the Lord and helped me to become selfless. I can honestly say that we are Spirit-led in our marriage today. Our marriage is a masterpiece, and yours can be too!

Chapter 4:

Masterpieces at Work and in the Community

Steven Furtick, pastor of Elevation Church in Charlotte, North Carolina, stated in one of his Christmas 2022 sermons that he read of something known as "the quiet quit" at work. This means that one doesn't quit his job; he is just absent in mind. He shows up, does his work half-heartedly, doesn't stay late, doesn't volunteer to take on any additional projects, leaves when it is time to leave... the "quiet quit." How many of us have done this or are starting to do this at work and in our lives in general?

God doesn't want us to be "quiet quitters" or quitters at all. In fact, the Word of God encourages us to do everything as unto the Lord, whole-heartedly.

In **I Corinthians 15: 58, the word of God declares, "Therefore, my dear brothers and sisters, stand firm. Let nothing move you. Always give yourselves fully to the work of the Lord, because you know that your labor in the Lord is not in vain."**

Now you may say, I Corinthians 15 is saying give yourselves fully to the work of the Lord, but that doesn't include my job. My work is secular; I don't work in the ministry. Ah, yes. **But Colossians 3: 17** says, "And whatever you do, whether in word or deed, do it all in the name of the Lord Jesus, giving thanks to God the Father through him." That means, "whatever work you do, do it all to the glory of God." Furthermore, it says in verse 18, "Wives, submit yourselves to your husbands, as is fitting in the Lord." This means, the work of a wife, is submission to her husband. Verse 19 says, "Husbands, love your wives and do not be harsh with them. The work of a husband is to love his wife. Even children are not exempt from work, they are to obey their parents in everything, according to verse 21 and finally, in verse 22, "Slaves are to obey their earthly masters in everything; and do it, not only when their eye is on you and to curry their favor, but with sincerity of heart and reverence for the Lord." Of course, we no longer have slaves today, but this is in reference to workers working for a boss or manager. Paul encourages us to work with "sincerity of heart." This means we should not be "quiet quitters" in our jobs, marriages, or relationships with our parents (even as adult children). Paul says in verse 23, "Whatever you do, work at it with all your heart, as working for the Lord, not for human masters." (I Corinthians 15 and Colossians 3:17-23, NIV).

If we do this, then we are being masterpieces at work, whether at our physical places of employment or our employment in the home. Yes, I will say it again, you are a masterpiece!

Masterpieces in the Community

Jesus encourages us to be servants. After all, He was a servant, and we are to be imitators of Christ. Don't believe me? Let's see what the Word of God has to say about servanthood.

In Luke 22, Jesus and His disciples were gathered around the table for the Last Supper and a dispute broke out among the disciples when he was exclaiming to them that he was going to be betrayed and must die. Verse 24 reads, "Then they began to argue among themselves about who would be the greatest among them. Jesus told them, 'In this world the kings and great men lord it over their people, yet they are called 'friends of the people.' But among you it will be different. Those who are the greatest among you should take the lowest rank and the leader should be like a servant. Who is more important, the one who sits at the table or the one who serves? The one who sits at the table, of course. But not here! For I am among you as one who serves" (Luke 22: 24-27, NLT).

We find in this passage, that our Savior takes the position of a servant and tells his followers that they must do the same. As we go out into the community, we must always remember to be servants. Although not biblical, Pastor Jimmy Evans of Gateway Church in Texas and founder of Marriage Today Ministries and XO Marriage, shares this picture:

"In heaven, there is a beautiful banquet table. All the food is laid out on the table with long, golden, and beautiful utensils attached to their hands and all the people are serving each other and everyone is eating to his heart's content. In hell, Evans says, there is also a beautiful banquet table. The food is laid out on the table, but all the people starve to death because they are not willing to serve one another."

What a sad image! We are commanded by our Savior to be servants. As masterpieces, we must serve in our community. There is a church in our neighborhood that captures this essence so well. It is a small church with barely over 50 members, but every Tuesday night from 5-6 p.m., they pass out groceries from local grocery stores. With inflation and the price of groceries being so high these days, they have really been a blessing to me and my husband. And we bring home so much food; we can give some away to our neighbors. The groceries are packaged so nicely, and they will even place it neatly in the backseat of your car. We come home, go through it, and keep what we need and then distribute the rest to our neighbors. My husband said, they serve us and bless us, we must share and serve to bless others.

This is what being a Masterpiece in your community is about. It is about giving, serving, and being a blessing to others!

Chapter 5:

You are a Winner

Because you are a masterpiece, you are a winner. If you didn't know this, just ask Pastor Joel Osteen. He wrote a book entitled, "You can, You Will" and in it, he said that we are winners. Even when you don't feel like you are a winner, you are. You are a carbon copy of God's DNA and if Jesus Christ is a winner, so are you! You must believe that you are a winner and declare it.

The other day, I woke up feeling defeated. I was doing a "no-no." Do you know what I was doing? I was comparing myself, my ministry, my calling, my body style, my entire life to someone else. This was a trick of the enemy. The Bible says, "Comparing yourselves among yourselves, is not wise." I know the word. Yet, I was doing it anyway. The devil had me at my heels and I had to decide whether I was going to give in to him or whether I was going to defeat him. Because I was doing all this "comparison," naturally I felt like a failure. I was trying to have a pity-party.

So, I decided right then and there that I wasn't going to give in to my "feelings and emotions." What did I do? I marched into the bathroom and declared war over my feelings and over Satan. I said, aloud (there is something powerful about saying it aloud): "Satan, I am not going to let you win! I am a winner in Jesus' name! I am the head and not the tail. I am above only and not beneath. No weapon formed against my mind today will prosper. You are trying to form these weapons against my thoughts, but they will not prevail. For greater is He who is in me than he who is in the world. I have the victory in Christ Jesus! I may not be like _____, (I said her name), but I am still just as strong, just as powerful, and just as mighty. " All of a sudden, the thoughts, just went away and a peace came over me and I heard the voice of the Holy Spirit in a still, small voice say: "This is my beloved child, in whom I am well-pleased."

Friends, I am telling you, you are a winner. When you feel defeated, lacking victory, depleted of energy, get your battle cry on, and go to war against the devil and your emotions. Pastors, authors, and theologians don't tell you this to make you feel good; it does work and you will feel better. There is power in speaking aloud and declaring who you are in Christ. You are a masterpiece!

...

Winners set goals and work to achieve them. How many people set New Year's Resolutions around the end of December and set out in January to accomplish their goals and then fail to achieve them by Jan. 31st because they get tired? Winners set goals and hang in there no matter what. Here are some tips from what I heard from an expert on Good Morning America about setting goals: "Make them Specific and Make them Seasonal, "the expert said.

 Each year, I set goals for the next year and achieve about half of them by December. This year, I decided to set my New Year's goals in terms. I made a shorter list and set them in terms according to the seasons from January- March; March-May; June-August; September-December. I also took the expert's advice and made my goals SMART this time: Specific, Measurable, Achievable, Realistic, and Timely.

SMART goals help incorporate these methods to make your goals easier to accomplish and achieve and more focused. **To make your goals "specific:" ask yourself the five "W" questions:**

1. Who is involved in this goal?

2. What do I want to accomplish?

3. Where is this goal to be achieved?

4. When do I want to achieve this goal?

5. Why do I want to achieve this goal?

For example, a general goal would be: "I want to get in shape." Which is what I normally said. This time, I said, "I want to start going to the local gym three days a week to be healthier and lose weight."

A SMART goal must be **measurable. It must have criteria for measuring progress. If there are no criteria, you will not** be able to determine your progress and whether you are on track for reaching your goal. To make your goal measurable, ask yourself:

1. How many/how much?

2. How do I know if I have reached my goal?

3. What is my indicator of progress?

Building on the above goal, I said: "I want to start going to my local gym three days a week to be healthier and lose weight. Every week, I will aim to lose 1 pound of body fat."

A SMART goal must be achievable and attainable. This will help you figure out ways you can work on that goal and attain it. It should stretch and challenge you. Ask yourself:

1. Do I have the resources and capabilities to achieve the goal? If not, what am I missing?

2. Have others achieved it successfully before?

Realistic SMART Goals

A SMART goal must be realistic in that the goal can be achieved in the time given and with the resources available. A SMART goal can be realistic if you believe it can be accomplished. Ask yourself:

1. Is the goal realistic and within a reasonable time?

2. Is the goal reachable with the resources available?

3. Am I able to commit to achieving the goal?

Timely SMART Goals

A SMART goal must be time-bound and have a start and finish date. If the SMART goal is not timely, there is no sense of urgency and you will likely not finish meeting the goal. For a SMART goal to be timely, ask yourself:

1. Does my goal have a deadline?

2. By what date or timeframe do I want to achieve my goal?

Building on the goal above, I said: "I want to go to my local gym three days a week to be healthier and get into shape and lose weight. I will do this by losing at least 1 pound of body fat a week. I will obtain the membership on January 1st, 2023 and I will know if I have met my goal if by January 31st, I am four lbs. lighter."

I realized that SMART Goals help make your life a little bit more defined and your goals a little bit more specific. I was taught this in college but needed a refresher.

I hope as you are on your journey to becoming a masterpiece, you will find this information enlightening.

The above information was taken from <u>SMART Goal - Definition, Guide, and Importance of Goal Setting (corporatefinanceinstitute. com)</u>.

Chapter 6

Understand your Anointing and Calling

Your anointing is what makes you unique- what makes you stand out from the crowd. When you show up in your anointing, those who you are called to hear you will come to you. It is like a symphony. If you are familiar with music, and you go to hear a symphony or an orchestra, if you played the clarinet or the flute in high school, you will naturally be drawn to hear those instruments at first when you are listening to the beautiful symphony or orchestra. In the same way, your anointing is the "song," the vibration that others hear when you speak, sing, teach, minister, or do whatever it is that you are called to do.

In the Greek, the definition for anointing was, *chrio (verb, Strong's Concordance 5548),* meaning "to anoint by rubbing or pouring olive oil" on someone to represent the empowering of the Holy Spirit. Anointing literally involved rubbing olive oil on the head, especially to present the individual as divinely authorized by God to serve as a prophet, priest, or king (see I Kings 19:16, Lev. 8:12, and I Sam. 10:1).

Webster's definition is like that of Strong's Concordance. It is: "to smear or rub an oily substance."

My definition is taken from Angelica Duncan, a women's online ministry consultant/minister who is the president and CEO of "Kingdom Influencer's Inner Circle." Her definition is: "To consecrate, set apart; chosen by God for a specific assignment or duty and as a result of being chosen, you're smeared with the supernatural ability to do natural things."

According to Mrs. Duncan, this is why you are specifically called not to mimic anyone else's anointing. When I first started ministry, I knew I had a call on my life, but I was not sure exactly what that call was. Many people told me that I was an evangelist, some told me I was called to be "just a teacher," others said I had a prophetic gift and was designed to be an intercessor. I knew that all these things were true to some extent, but I needed God to clarify for me, what exactly my calling was for His service. As I went through different seasons of hurt and pain and growth in life, I have discovered, that the purpose of my life is as follows:

"To sow seeds into the lives of others, encouraging them to fulfill their God-given destiny. I will carry out this mission by educating, counseling, coaching, mentoring, leading, and teaching others, particularly the Body of Christ; and eventually develop an online Christian-based education ministry for children and adults, with my ultimate goal of becoming an international motivational speaker and writer."

So, what has God called you to do? What is God's purpose for your life? We already know that you are a masterpiece, but perhaps you are not sure what God has called you to do here on the earth. Perhaps you are like me and have a lot of gifts and talents and don't know how to channel them and narrow your focus. I encourage you to ask yourself the following questions on your quest to find and follow what God has called you to do:

1. List your talents, gifts, skills, and expertise.

2. What are your spiritual gifts?

3. What area do you flow in with ease?

4. What area do people come to you and seek your counsel or advice on?

5. What drives you and keeps you up at night and fuels your passion?

6. Where have people said your bring transformation into their lives?

After you have answered these questions, you have probably found out what you are called to do. Remember, your calling is a "what" and a "to whom."

Our calling is a command wrapped in an invitation. Your calling cannot be fulfilled without an anointing. Your anointing is your specialty area and your calling is "to that" and "to whom." For example, a physician is called to be a "doctor" and then there are different types of doctors who specialize in certain areas such as neurology, ob/gyn, cardiology, etc. I hope you are following what I am saying. You can't miss your calling. One can be in jail and still fulfill their purpose. For example, look at Joseph in the Bible. Joseph was called from his youth to be save his brothers and father from famine in Egypt. Even though he was thrown into a pit, thrown into jail, and forgotten about by the chief baker for a while, he still fulfilled his purpose. Am I right? Read the story for yourself in Genesis 37: 12-36; 39,40, 41-45. God sent Joseph to Egypt to deliver his family from famine and he became second in command of all of Egypt. His dreams came to pass, and his brothers bowed down to him.

So, I ask you again, what are you called to do? Are there dreams and visions that God has placed in your heart, but you are sitting on them because you are waiting for some magical moment to appear, or a genie to whisk you off and help you fulfill your purpose? If God has placed a dream, a calling in your spirit, then it is time to recognize your *Karios* moment and fulfill it… because you are a masterpiece!

Chapter 7

Enhance your imagination

In his book, *Your Best Life Now*, author and pastor Joel Osteen tells a story in the first chapter about a man who is out on vacation with his wife in Hawaii. The tour guide takes them to see a beautiful house on an island, and the man says aloud and to himself something to the effect of, "Oh, boy I don't think I could ever own or live in a house like that." Then he hears a voice say, "Yep, and you never will." And he says, "Well, what do you mean?" And the voice inside replies, "Well, if you can't see it, you can't believe it or achieve it."

The man determined right then and there that he had to enlarge his vision of what God could and would do in and through his life. Joel goes on to explain we must imagine ourselves living as the victor and achieving our destiny.

And I have found this to be so true. I've read this book three times and am now reading it for the fourth time! It has had such a profound impact on me. I would like to stop right now and say, "What are you putting in your imagination? "As my favorite Oversight pastor, Bishop L.W. Francisco III of C3 Hampton often says, "You have to change the nation of your imagination." Are you picturing yourself as the victor or the one being defeated? Perhaps you got a bad medical report, or your child is being bullied and you feel like everyone always picks on you and your family. How are you imagining the outcome in these situations? Are you saying, "As Christ is my witness, my King Jesus took upon Himself stripes for my healing and by His stripes, I am healed. My family is the head and not the tail, and we are not defeated; my child will not be bullied by naysayers….?" Do you imagine yourself succeeding?

The Bible says we must watch what we put before our eye and ear gates. In a few months, I am going to take a mental health coaching and professional life coaching exam to receive my mental health and professional life coaching certification with AACC (American Association of Christian Counselors) Over the past three weeks, I have been saying, "I am going to pass the test on my first attempt. I am a Board-Certified Mental Health and Professional Life Coach in Jesus's name!" I have been imagining myself sitting at the computer answering each question with confidence and boldness that I will receive a score of 80% or higher. That image has stayed ingrained in my psyche. And I am telling you, that is what you must do when God has given you a vision or dream. You must imagine the best.

 When I was a freshman in high school, I was placed in the low English class by my guidance counselor. My English teacher began to realize that I was falling asleep in class because I was bored, and the classwork was not challenging enough for me. I needed to be placed in the college-prep class. When I went to the guidance counselor, the guidance counselor told me that I would probably make "D's" in this college-prep class, but it would be equivalent to an "A-"or "B+" because the course was weighted heavier. This infuriated me. My teacher believed in me, but the guidance counselor did not. So, I told her to place me in the class anyway because I wanted to try it.

The second grading term ended and I received an "A- "on my report card in the college- prep class. I ran to the guidance counselor's office and burst in, and she said, "Deanna, you don't have an appointment, what do you need?" And I said, "Oh, I won't be long. I just wanted to show you my A- on my report card for my college-prep English class for this second nine weeks and I wanted to tell you that next nine weeks, I plan to make an A+." She was shocked. Here she was trying to prophesy over me a low grade and I wasn't having it. I was determined to prove her wrong. I imagined and conceived in my heart the next nine weeks that I could make a "A" and I did! I would like to report that when the third nine weeks report card came out, I did make an "A+" and continued to earn "A+" throughout the remainder of my terms in my English high school career. Hallelujah!

When you conceive and imagine something, there is no devil in hell that can stop you. The Bible exclaims, "Greater is He that is within you, than he who is in the world." I am living proof of it, Masterpieces!

Therefore, what are you imagining? What is in your psyche? As I am writing this chapter of the book, I am recovering from back surgery. Yes, back surgery! Everyone told me not to have it. But the Holy Spirit spoke to my spirit and said, "Have the back surgery in July, it is the way I plan to heal your back." You see, I had been going through back pain for the past year and it was only intensifying. I had to quit my jobs as a mental health professional and as a substitute teacher because of it. I tried physical therapy (both on land and aqua), epidurals, chiropractor, massage therapy... and nothing was working. It got to the point where I could no longer walk without a walker. I had gone to the altar for prayer on numerous occasions, but to no avail. But when you get a word from the Holy Spirit and conceive something in your imagination, there is nothing too hard for God! I knew that this surgery was not going to be like my back surgery in 2018, I saw and imagined myself healed and walking. I am happy to report, now three weeks later, I can walk up and down the stairs in my townhome with no problem, down the street (safely alone with my walker) and all over my townhome with no walker at all! God is good! And He told me that I would be all right and this was the way to my healing. I am a Masterpiece, in Jesus' name!

And so are you! Receive it into your spirit man right now. Wherever you are, cry out loud, "I AM A MASTERPIECE, IN JESUS NAME, AMEN!"

Chapter 8:

Conclusion

We have covered a lot of ground in these seven chapters, but I want to tell you that I believe by the power of the Holy Spirit, some of you were healed and transformed or at least reminded of your position in Christ. I hope that you will walk in your fullness and dominion and divine purpose in the Lord, and if you don't know your purpose, I pray you will search diligently for it by continuing to do self-reflection exercises, spiritual gift inventories, personality inventories, and most importantly, seeking God's face and hearing His voice for clarity and direction. I love and thank everyone who is reading this book right now, and I declare by the power of the Holy Spirit: YOU ARE A MASTERPIECE!

Thank you for purchasing this book, and be blessed as you look forward to reading future writings from me.

Acknowledgements

want to thank my two aunts who always support me: Joyce Cunningham, and my aunt D. Laverne Johnson who always edits my books and prays with me when I am discouraged. My husband, Louis Moses who is my best friend and loves me unconditionally, cries with me, encourages me, supports me and is always there for me. My mother, father, stepmother, sister, and niece who are also cheerleaders in the background. My church family and all my pastors who have shaped me and molded me into the strong Christian woman of faith that I am today and of course, my Lord and Savior Jesus Christ. I am nothing without Him! Love you all.